First Printing, 2018
Wild Cabbage Books
wildcabbagebooks.com

> I'm trying to fight

I'm trying to
fight

Each of us is limitless; each of us with his
or her right upon the earth.

— Walt Whitman

> This above all: to thine ownself be true.
>
> — Shakespeare

Excellence is not an act, but a habit.

— Aristotle

No act of kindness, no matter how small, is ever wasted.
— Aesop

> The way to be happy is to make others so.
>
> — Robert Ingersoll

> Be happy for this moment. This moment is your life.
>
> — Omar Kayyam

> Peace is always beautiful.
>
> – Walt Whitman

> The greatest mistake you can make in life is to be continually fearing you will make one.
>
> – Elbert Hubbard

Bloom where you are planted.

— 1 Corinthians KJV

Manufactured by Amazon.ca
Bolton, ON